NYC Cocktails

NYC Cocktails

Kathryn Maier
Illustrations by Sarah Campbell

Smith Street Books

The Cocktails of New York City

New York is a cocktail city. It always has been.

What is a New York City cocktail? You might as well just say "cocktail". After all, it was here (or, rather, in the nearby small town of Hudson) where the word "cocktail" first appeared in print, in a newspaper article in 1806, describing what we'd now call an Old Fashioned.

It was in New York City that Jerry Thomas, author of the first cocktail book published in the U.S. and the "father of American mixology", primarily lived and plied his trade. It was also here that a number of hotel bars and private clubs (most notably The Waldorf-Astoria) gave rise to countless cocktails in the 19th and early 20th centuries, many of which are detailed in these pages.

And it was in New York City that "King Cocktail" Dale DeGroff resurrected these classics in the 1980s and '90s while bartending at the Rainbow Room, redirecting the genre from carelessly made mixed drinks to carefully crafted cocktails using fresh ingredients. When Sasha Petraske took things a notch further in 2000 with the opening of Milk & Honey, the seminal proto-modern cocktail bar that changed the way we drink today ... well, that was in New York City, too.

Since then, cocktails have reigned supreme in New York, perhaps more so than in any other city in the world. There's a craft cocktail bar on seemingly every corner, and it's tough to find a restaurant, from a pizza joint to a taco spot, that doesn't offer a full cocktail menu and can't whip up a world-class Negroni or Margarita.

Many of the most prolific creators of modern-classic cocktails—Sam Ross, Joaquín Simó, and Phil Ward, to name but a few—call the city home.

The pages that follow will spotlight the people and places that have made New York City the best drinking city in America over the past 100-plus years.

So we return to the question: What is a New York City cocktail? By the simplest definition, it's one that was created here, whether in pre-Prohibition times or much more recently, or one that has become so closely associated with the city that it might as well have been birthed within its five boroughs.

It could also be the first drink a new resident stirred up in their first New York City apartment, the most memorable drink someone had during their first visit to the city, or the one most frequently consumed at the liveliest brunches in the West Village. In short, it's the cocktail that makes you think of the city fondly, even when you're away, or even if you've never been.

You're sure to discover a favorite New York City cocktail of your own in these pages.

Setting Up Your Home Bar

Making a cocktail is a simple matter of following a recipe. You can set yourself up for the most success, however, by having a few necessary items on hand.

These are the essential bar tools and glassware for making—and enjoying—cocktails.

EQUIPMENT

Cocktail shaker

A metal container for making shaken drinks. The two-tin style is commonly used in bars, but novice drink-makers may prefer the easier-to-use cobbler style, with its built-in strainer.

Mixing glass

A glass (ideally with a spout) that can hold liquid and ice for making stirred cocktails.

Barspoon

A spoon with a long and often twisted handle, used for stirring cocktails.

Strainer

A strainer keeps ice and any other solids out of your cocktail when pouring from a shaker or mixing glass. A hawthorne strainer has a coil and is typically used with the two-tin style of shaker. A julep strainer is typically used with a mixing glass.

Jigger

A measuring device, often double-ended, for measuring quantities of ingredients.

Muddler

A blunt stick-like tool used for releasing flavor from herbs, fruits, and other non-liquid ingredients.

GLASSWARE

Rocks glass

A short, squat glass for cocktails served "on the rocks", or over ice.

Collins glass

A tall and straight-sided glass, ideal for drinks served "long", or with a substantial carbonated element. A Highball glass is similar, but slightly shorter and wider. The two can be used somewhat interchangeably.

Coupe

A stemmed glass with a wide bowl, used for serving drinks "up", or without ice.

Martini glass

The standard V-shaped stemmed glass that probably comes to mind when you think of a Martini.

Nick & Nora

An elegant stemmed glass with a taller and narrower bowl than a coupe, generally used for spirit-forward drinks served "up", such as Martinis, Manhattans, and variations thereupon.

Flute

A tall, slender, stemmed glass often used for serving Champagne or other sparkling wine—as well as cocktails that include sparkling wine.

Hurricane

A tall, curvy glass with a short stem, used for serving many tiki-style drinks.

Snifter

A bulbous glass with a short stem, often used for serving brandy, dessert wines, or other highly aromatic drinks.

In general, if you don't want to devote an entire cupboard to glassware, any cocktail that calls for a martini glass or Nick & Nora glass can instead be served in a coupe, in a pinch.

For drinks served "up" (which is to say, not over ice), it's particularly nice to use a glass that's been chilled. You can either chill the glasses in the freezer for 30 minutes in advance, or fill them with water and crushed ice as you're making the drinks.

SPIRITS, LIQUEURS, & SUCH

There are different styles within each main spirit category, and it's important to appreciate their unique qualities. Indeed, every brand will have nuances of its own.

Generally, in a real pinch, you can use a different brand or style within a given category. Keep in mind, however, that a cocktail's creator chooses each ingredient for the specific characteristics it possesses and the way it interplays with the cocktail's other ingredients—so using a different brand or style than the one called for in a recipe may mean your cocktail tastes different to how its creator intended.

Gin

For the cocktails in this book, the London dry style—the juniper-forward style of most well-known brands—is intended, unless otherwise specified. Plymouth is both a brand and a style of gin, softer than London dry. Old Tom is yet another style, sweeter and fuller-bodied (look for Hayman's). And, finally, there's sloe gin, flavored with sloe berries to produce a sweet, tart, liqueur-ish style.

Whiskey

This spirit comes in various forms: bourbon and its spicier cousin, rye, plus those typically denoted by country: Irish, Scotch, and so on. Whiskey has a wide range of flavors resulting from the use of different grains and various methods of distilling.

Rum

Aged rum is darker and more flavorful than unaged or light/white rum. Flavors vary widely based on the country or island of origin. Jamaican rum generally possesses funky notes, whereas Haitian rum has grassy ones, for instance, which is why a specific country's rum will sometimes be called for in a recipe.

Tequila and mezcal

Look for tequilas made with 100 per cent blue weber agave. Blanco tequilas are unaged and great for making cocktails containing citrus. Reposado is barrel-aged and lovely in Old Fashioned–style cocktails, or for sipping on its own. Mezcal is made from a wide range of agave types, with an equally wide range of resulting flavors.

Vodka

Use whatever's handy; no one's judging.

Vermouth

This fortified wine comes in two main styles: dry (white and primarily French), and sweet (red and generally Italian). Dolin is the most commonly used brand of dry vermouth. Recommended brands of sweet vermouth include Carpano Antica and Cocchi Vermouth di Torino. Bianco/blanc vermouth is white and French, but sweet; when that style is needed, it will be specifically noted.

Keep vermouth refrigerated after opening the bottle; it will eventually go "off", just as a bottle of wine will, albeit more slowly.

Liqueurs

Made from a base spirit, sweetened, and flavored with fruits, flowers, and/or herbs, liqueurs are often used in very small quantities. Commonly used ones include Cointreau, a premium triple sec (orange-flavored liqueur) that is less sweet than most, and Luxardo maraschino liqueur, a different thing entirely from the syrup in a jar of cherries.

Amaro

These bitter liqueurs, often Italian, are delicious sipped on their own as well as in cocktails, once you get accustomed to their strong flavors. Use the specific one named in the recipe whenever possible. Amari have a wide range of flavors, and they are generally not interchangeable with each other without significantly altering a cocktail's flavor.

Bitters

These concentrated flavoring agents are, with one notable exception (see the Trinidad Sour, page 96), meant to be used in tiny amounts. The most commonly called for is Angostura—meaning the original aromatic type (with the yellow cap), with its notes of wintery baking spices. Orange bitters are often used as well; most New York City bartenders usually reach for Regans' Orange Bitters No. 6, created by NYC cocktail legend Gary ("Gaz") Regan. Other bitters are noted where appropriate. Beyond their use in cocktails, bitters are also tasty when added to unflavored seltzer or soda water.

MIXERS & GARNISHES

Fruit juice

When a recipe calls for fruit juice (most often citrus such as lemon or lime), freshly squeezed with the aid of a juicer is always best. The one exception is pineapple juice, for which the canned variety is preferred for both convenience and consistency.

Carbonation

When a carbonated ingredient such as soda water, sparkling wine, or ginger beer is called for, never shake it along with the other ingredients. Shake all other ingredients first and strain them into your glass, then add the carbonated element afterward, stirring the drink gently and briefly with a barspoon to combine.

Syrups

Particularly for cocktails containing citrus, a sweet element is necessary for balancing the flavors. You'll find recipes for syrups toward the end of this book. These will generally produce much more syrup than is required for a cocktail or two; feel free to halve the quantities if desired. Always cool the syrup to room temperature (or below) before using it in a cocktail, keeping any extra tightly sealed and refrigerated for later use.

Ice

The smaller ice cubes produced in a standard ice cube tray, about 1 inch (2.5 cm) cubed, are fine to shake with, and are good in drinks served "on the rocks" as well. (Always use fresh ice in the drink; never reuse the ice that was used to shake or stir the ingredients.)

Spirit-forward cocktails are often served over one large ice cube, about 2 inches (5 cm) cubed, as large ice cubes melt more slowly and will not overdilute your drink.

Pebble or crushed ice is great for tropical-style drinks.

Twists

Citrus twists are the most common garnishes, and they should always be expressed over the drink (see "How to garnish", opposite) before dropping them into the glass.

Cocktail cherries

When a cocktail cherry is called for, a brandied or high-quality maraschino cherry is meant (the best-known brand being Luxardo)—*not* the bright-red things that typically sit atop an ice-cream sundae.

MIXING A COCKTAIL

Shaking or stirring doesn't simply combine the drink's ingredients; it performs the necessary functions of chilling and diluting the drink as well. Shaking also aerates the drink, so that creamy drinks froth and the sharp acidity of citrus gets rounded out by the tiny bubbles produced. In general, if the cocktail includes citrus, egg white, or a dairy element such as cream, it should be shaken. Otherwise, it should be stirred to produce a smoother, silkier texture.

How to shake

Add your ingredients to a cocktail shaker, then add enough ice cubes to fill it halfway. Close the shaker and shake vigorously, with a mostly lateral motion toward your shoulder (rather than up and down), for 15–20 seconds. You'll feel the shaker get a bit frosty; this is the sign that the drink is sufficiently chilled.

To shake a drink made with egg white, add your ingredients to the shaker—*without ice*—and shake vigorously, making sure the shaker is tightly sealed (it sometimes leaks during this step). This is often referred to as a "dry shake". Open the shaker and add ice, then shake again for 20 seconds more.

How to stir

Add your ingredients to a mixing glass, then add enough ice cubes to fill the glass about halfway or two-thirds full. Stir by running your long-handled barspoon around the inner wall of the glass for about 20–30 seconds, keeping the back of the spoon against the glass. You're doing it right if the ice is nearly silent as it spins within the mixing glass.

How to garnish

When a citrus twist is called for, use a Y-peeler to get a strip of citrus peel about 1 inch (2.5 cm) wide. Express the natural citrus oils by holding the twist about an inch or two above the drink, skin side down, and squeezing. You can then drop the twist into the drink to garnish.

When citrus wedges or wheels are called for, these are best perched on the side of the glass. Feel free to squeeze them into the cocktail before drinking, if you like.

When garnishing with a cherry, olive, or onion, it's best to first skewer it on a cocktail pick, to make it easier to fish the garnish out of the glass and nibble on later.

How to muddle

Add the ingredient(s) to be muddled into the vessel in which the cocktail will be made, and use a muddler to gently press about five times. Don't be overly aggressive, as this can actually dampen fruit flavors or release bitter ones from herbs.

A FINAL NOTE, BEFORE YOU BEGIN...

All the recipes in this book produce one cocktail. To make two of the same cocktail, simply double the ingredient quantities. To make more than two cocktails, it's best to make multiple batches; overloading a shaker or mixing glass with ingredients works about as well as overloading a clothes dryer—which is to say, the outcome might not be as good as desired.

The Early Years

Pre–1900

MANHATTAN

MARTINI

OLD FASHIONED

TOM COLLINS

NEW YORK SOUR

BIJOU

METROPOLE

CLOVER CLUB

ADONIS

PERFECT MARTINI

SHERRY COBBLER

ROB ROY

WEEPER'S JOY

GIN & IT

ORDER #111294

Possibly the most New York City of all cocktails (it's even named for the city's best-known borough), the Manhattan was first stirred up sometime in the late 1800s, when vermouth was first gaining popularity among bartenders. As with many old cocktails, its exact provenance is uncertain, but the most popular theory names its origin as the Manhattan Club and pinpoints its creation as somewhere between the 1860s and the 1880s.

This drink spawned many successors, most notably the Brooklyn (page 48) and that cocktail's many spinoffs.

Manhattan

Add all the ingredients to a mixing glass with ice and stir until well-chilled. Strain into a coupe or Nick & Nora glass. Garnish with a cocktail cherry and/or a lemon twist, as desired.

2 oz (60 ml) rye whiskey (preferably Rittenhouse)

1 oz (30 ml) sweet vermouth (preferably Carpano Antica or Cocchi Vermouth di Torino)

2 dashes Angostura bitters

GARNISH

Cocktail cherry and/or lemon twist

DOLIN DOL
ROUGE
DOLIN
Maison fondée en 1821
VERMOUTH
DE
CHAMBÉRY

The Martini's true origin is unknown. Many say it was first created in New York City, some argue it originated elsewhere. Regardless, this classic is now as much a part of NYC as bagels or pigeons.

It's an infinitely customizable cocktail. Use the recipe below as a starting point and alter it as you wish. Gin or vodka are both acceptable, and you can add as much or as little vermouth as you prefer. Splash in a bit of olive brine to make it "dirty", as is currently trendy in the city, if you like. Just remember that James Bond didn't know best when it comes to cocktails: This drink should be stirred, never shaken.

Martini

Add the gin or vodka and dry vermouth (and bitters or olive brine, if using) to a mixing glass with ice and stir until well-chilled. Strain into a martini glass. Garnish with cocktail olives and/or a lemon twist, as desired.

2 oz (60 ml) London dry gin (or vodka)

1 oz (30 ml) dry vermouth

2 dashes orange bitters (optional)

Olive brine, to taste (optional)

GARNISH

Cocktail olives and/or lemon twist

BOURBON
WHISKEY
BOURBON
WHISKEY

This drink is, essentially, the original cocktail; its ingredients (spirit, sugar, water, and bitters) given as the definition for the word in a newspaper in 1806.

The Old Fashioned has been endlessly riffed upon over the decades, but its simplest and most classic version—the recipe given here—remains a favorite among cocktail enthusiasts. It's crucial to choose a good whiskey for this drink, since the whiskey's flavor will shine through strongly in this otherwise simple drink.

Old Fashioned

Add the sugar cube and bitters to a mixing glass and gently muddle. Add the whiskey and ice and stir until well-chilled. Strain into a rocks glass over one large ice cube. Garnish with an orange twist.

1 sugar cube

2 dashes Angostura bitters

2 oz (60 ml) bourbon or rye whiskey

GARNISH

Orange twist

This drink likely derived from the punches being served in London at the time; a bartender there named John Collins had created a similar cocktail, apparently around the mid-19th century, and named it after himself.

That cocktail came to the States not long after and got its new name from, supposedly, a hoax circulating through New York City in 1874. A prankster would tell a friend that a certain Tom Collins had been besmirching his name at a local bar, and that his affronted friend should find this Mr. Collins and give him a what-for. Some enterprising bartender who was asked for the fictional "Tom Collins" one too many times apparently created this riff on the John Collins in response. Its recipe first appeared in print two years later in Jerry Thomas' *The Bartender's Guide*.

Tom Collins

Add the gin, lemon juice, and syrup to a Collins or highball glass. Add ice, then top with soda water. Stir gently and briefly to combine. Garnish with a lemon wheel and cocktail cherry, if desired.

2 oz (60 ml) gin

1 oz (30 ml) lemon juice, freshly squeezed

½ oz (15 ml) Simple Syrup (see page 163)

Soda water, to top

GARNISH

Lemon wheel and cocktail cherry (optional)

BATCH
GIN
UNFILTERED
Distilled with
star anise $
lemon myrtle

Admittedly, this drink is said to have originated in Chicago in the 1880s, but it only acquired its current name after it migrated to New York City and gained fame and popularity there.

The cocktail is essentially a classic whiskey sour, with the twist that red wine is carefully "floated" over the drink, creating a layered effect and adding fruity, earthy notes to each sip. It's delicious either with or without egg white, which adds a foamy texture and frothy top to the drink.

New York Sour

- 1 egg white (optional)
- 2 oz (60 ml) bourbon or rye whiskey
- 1 oz (30 ml) lemon juice, freshly squeezed
- ¾ oz (20 ml) Simple Syrup (see page 163)
- ½ oz (15 ml) red wine (ideally a bolder and fruit-forward wine, such as cabernet sauvignon)

GARNISH

Lemon twist (optional)

If using egg white, add all the ingredients except the red wine to a cocktail shaker, without ice, and shake vigorously until frothy (about 20 seconds). Open the shaker and add ice, and vigorously shake again until well-chilled.

If not using egg white, add all the ingredients except the red wine to a shaker with ice and shake until well-chilled.

Strain into a rocks glass over ice. Place a spoon over the glass, facing downward, with the tip just touching the liquid, and slowly pour the red wine over the back of the spoon so that it layers on top of the liquid. Garnish with a lemon twist, if desired.

CHARTREUSE
LIQUEUR FABRIQUÉE
PAR LES PÈRES
CHARTREUX
1605
L. Garnier

The earliest version of this jewel of a drink appeared in Harry Johnson's *Bartender's Manual*, published in 1882 while Johnson was bartending in New York City. That version of the cocktail called for an equal-parts formula, but these days most fans of the drink enjoy it with slightly altered proportions.

The Bijou is an aptly named cocktail: Elegant and many-faceted, it will leave you sparkling.

Bijou

Add all the ingredients to a mixing glass with ice and stir until well-chilled. Strain into a coupe or Nick & Nora glass. Garnish with a cocktail cherry or an orange twist, as desired.

1½ oz (45 ml) gin

¾ oz (20 ml) green Chartreuse

¾ oz (20 ml) sweet vermouth

2 dashes orange bitters

GARNISH

Cocktail cherry or orange twist

Created in the late 1800s, this cocktail was the house drink at the Hotel Metropole, a seedy Times Square landmark with a cafe where folks of ill repute would gather at all hours of the night. The hotel closed in 1912, following the murder of a notorious casino boss just outside its doors and the scandal that ensued, but the drink bearing its name lives on.

This version, slightly updated from the original, comes courtesy of Frank Caiafa, who formerly helmed the bar at The Waldorf-Astoria.

Metropole

Combine all the ingredients in a mixing glass with ice and stir until well-chilled. Strain into a Nick & Nora glass. Garnish with a lemon twist and/or cocktail cherry, as desired.

2 oz (60 ml) Cognac

1 oz (30 ml) dry vermouth

½ oz (15 ml) Simple Syrup (see page 163)

2 dashes Peychaud's bitters

1 dash orange bitters

GARNISH

Lemon twist and/or cocktail cherry

This cocktail hails from Philadelphia, where it's thought to have been created in the late 1800s before making its way to bars in New York City. After the Prohibition era, however, the drink was largely forgotten.

A pioneering Brooklyn cocktail bar that opened in 2008, helmed by Julie Reiner, not only helped resurrect the cocktail, but also borrowed its name. The recipe below is the one Reiner and her team use at Clover Club.

Clover Club

Add all the ingredients to a cocktail shaker without ice and shake vigorously for about 20 seconds. Open the shaker and add ice, then shake again until well-chilled. Strain into a coupe glass. Garnish with three raspberries skewered on a cocktail pick.

1½ oz (45 ml) gin

½ oz (15 ml) dry vermouth

½ oz (15 ml) lemon juice, freshly squeezed

½ oz (15 ml) Raspberry Syrup (see page 162)

1 egg white

GARNISH

3 raspberries, skewered

PLYMOUTH GIN
CRAFTED IN ENGLAND
750 ml BATCH-DISTILLED 41.2%
Original Strength

Fragata
STONELESS
GREEN
OLIVES

Adonis opened in New York City in 1894 and was the first Broadway musical to run for more than 500 performances. The cocktail named for the production was created at the Hoffman House hotel to honor that milestone.

Featuring sherry and sweet vermouth, both of which generally clock in at around just 15% ABV, this low-alcohol drink makes an ideal pre-dinner aperitif—perfect for whetting your appetite without encouraging you to mistake yourself or your dining companion for a Greek god.

Adonis

Combine all the ingredients in a mixing glass with ice and stir until well-chilled. Strain into a Nick & Nora glass. Garnish with an orange twist and/or cocktail olive, as desired.

2 oz (60 ml) fino sherry

1 oz (30 ml) sweet vermouth

2 dashes orange bitters

GARNISH

Orange twist and/or cocktail olive

The forerunner to the now-standard Martini employed sweet vermouth instead of the dry style currently used. The Perfect Martini—not to be confused with an "ideal" Martini, whatever that means to you—splits the difference between the old Martini style and the contemporary one, employing half sweet vermouth and half dry in "perfect" proportions.

It's a drink that fell out of favor for decades but is once again fashionable in New York City, being served at spots such as Tigre and Gage & Tollner.

Perfect Martini

Add all the ingredients to a mixing glass with ice and stir until well-chilled. Strain into a coupe or martini glass. Garnish with a lemon twist.

2 oz (60 ml) gin

½ oz (15 ml) dry vermouth

½ oz (15 ml) sweet vermouth

2 dashes Angostura or orange bitters (optional)

GARNISH

Lemon twist

REGANS'
Orange Bitt
№ 6

This drink is so old its name appears in Dickens' *The Life and Adventures of Martin Chuzzlewit*, where it is called a "wonderful invention". The first written reference to it predates even that, appearing in the 1838 diary of an Englishwoman who encountered the drink in New York City.

Countless variations exist. Use the recipe below as a starting point, and feel free to experiment with proportions or seasonal fruits or even different types of sherry. Two elements are mandatory, however: crushed or pebble ice and a festive garnish. Go wild!

Sherry Cobbler

Add all the ingredients to a cocktail shaker with ice and shake vigorously to muddle the orange slices. Strain into a highball or hurricane glass filled with crushed or pebble ice. Garnish as desired. Serve with a straw.

3 oz (90 ml) amontillado sherry

¼ oz (10 ml) Luxardo maraschino liqueur or Simple Syrup (see page 163)

2 orange slices

GARNISH

Seasonal fruit, mint sprig, or anything you prefer

LUXARDO
Zara 1821
1947 Torregia
LIQUEUR
GIROLAMO LUXARDO
IN TORREGLIA
MARASCHINO
AMONTILLADO
DEL ZULA
SHERRY
AGED 12 YEARS
75 cle

VERMOUTH

Created in the bar of The Waldorf-Astoria, this descendant of the Manhattan cocktail was named after a romantic comic operetta that opened in New York City in 1894. The operetta was loosely based on the life of Robert Roy MacGregor, the Scottish folk hero and subject of the Sir Walter Scott novel.

The drink is a proper choice for enjoying before or after paying one's respects to the statue of Sir Scott that stands at the beginning of the Literary Walk in Central Park.

Rob Roy

Add all the ingredients to a mixing glass with ice and stir until well-chilled. Strain into a coupe or Nick & Nora glass. Garnish with a lemon twist or cocktail cherry, as desired.

2 oz (60 ml) blended Scotch whisky

1 oz (30 ml) sweet vermouth (preferably Carpano Antica)

2 dashes orange bitters or Angostura bitters

GARNISH

Lemon twist or cocktail cherry

This unusual cocktail was created by New York City bartender William Schmidt, the first bartender to be renowned for creating his own cocktails—which he did prolifically. First published in Schmidt's 1892 cocktail book *The Flowing Bowl*, the original recipe called for equal parts kummel (a sweet herbal liqueur), absinthe, and sweet vermouth, with a splash of orange liqueur and a touch of gomme syrup (a rich simple syrup with gum arabic added).

NYC's famed bar The Dead Rabbit has updated the mix to be more in line with modern tastes. The result: A cocktail that's pronouncedly herbaceous and as dry as a New Yorker's wit.

Weeper's Joy

Combine all the ingredients in a mixing glass with ice and stir until well-chilled. Strain into a Nick & Nora glass. Express the oils from the orange twist over the drink, then discard the twist.

NOTE

The celery shrub is a specialty ingredient. In New York City, it is carried at Astor Wines & Spirits. For those elsewhere, it can be ordered online via Bitters & Bottles, among other retailers.

- 2 oz (60 ml) dry vermouth
- ¾ oz (20 ml) kummel
- ¼ oz (10 ml) Bénédictine
- ½ oz (15 ml) absinthe (preferably Pernod)
- 3 dashes Bittermens Orchard Street Celery Shrub (see Note)
- 3 dashes orange bitters

GARNISH

Orange twist

QUALITÉ
1805
Recette Traditionnelle
DISTILLÉE EN FRANCE
A BASE D'ALCOOL DE VIN

Known in the 1880s as a "sweet Martini" (the "It" in the name refers to Italian or sweet red vermouth), this cocktail's recipe has undergone as much of an evolution as its name. In the 1905 *Hoffman House Bartender's Guide* (from the Hoffman House hotel in New York City), it originally called for a heavier gin-to-vermouth ratio, and was served at room temperature. Modern drinkers will prefer to stir it over ice.

The version below was a favorite sip of the late Sasha Petraske, the founder of the groundbreaking NYC bar Milk & Honey.

Gin & It

Combine the gin and vermouth in a mixing glass with ice and stir until well-chilled. Strain into a Nick & Nora glass. Garnish with a lemon twist.

2 oz (60 ml) gin

1 oz (30 ml) sweet vermouth

GARNISH

Lemon twist

COCCHI
STORICO
VERMOUTH DI TORINO
RICETTA ORIGINALE

Cocktails Get Going

1900–1920

NEGRONI

BROOKLYN

AVIATION

GIBSON

TUXEDO #2

FRENCH 75

BRONX

SOUTHSIDE

CHARLIE CHAPLIN

TIPPERARY

JACK ROSE

(BRANDY) ALEXANDER

— THANK YOU —

The Negroni was first stirred up more than a century ago in Florence, Italy. These days, a Negroni (or a spin thereupon) appears on nearly every bar menu throughout New York City, and for good reason. Perhaps no cocktail better exemplifies NYC: notably bitter, a tiny bit pretentiously intellectual, with a down-to-earth sweetness deep within. People either love it or hate it; there's no in-between.

Countless variations of the cocktail exist, but it's best to start with the most classic version, which is the recipe below.

Negroni

Add all the ingredients to a mixing glass with ice and stir until well-chilled. Strain into a rocks glass over one large ice cube. Garnish with an orange twist.

1 oz (30 ml) gin

1 oz (30 ml) Campari

1 oz (30 ml) sweet vermouth

GARNISH

Orange twist

CAMPARI
SINCE 1860
CAMPARI
Davide Campari
MILANO
BITTER

The Brooklyn descended from the Manhattan cocktail very early in the 20th century. It hasn't truly been seen in the States since the 1960s, however, when Amer Picon, a French aperitif and an essential component of the drink, became unavailable here.

Various cocktail experts have devised substitutes for Amer Picon. Some suggest a mixture of half Ramazzotti amaro and half orange bitters. Some simply use Amaro CioCiaro or Bigallet China-China Amer, or even just a couple of dashes of Angostura bitters. Or you might skip replicating it and simply move on to any of the Brooklyn riffs that have arisen in recent years that sidestep Amer Picon entirely, such as the Bensonhurst cocktail on page 114.

Brooklyn

Add all the ingredients to a mixing glass with ice and stir until well-chilled. Strain into a coupe glass. Garnish with a cocktail cherry, if desired.

- 2 oz (60 ml) rye whiskey
- ½ oz (15 ml) dry vermouth
- ¼ oz (10 ml) Amer Picon (or various substitutes, named above)
- ¼ oz (10 ml) maraschino liqueur (preferably Luxardo)

GARNISH

Cocktail cherry (optional)

PICON
BIÈRE
APÉRITIF AU CITRON
DEPUIS 1837
cl
18% vol

HENDRICK'S
BRIOTTET
Liqueur de
Violette
FRANCE
18% vol
HENDRICK'S
DISTILLED and BOTTLED IN SCOTLAND
GIN
EST 1886

The Aviation first appeared in print in New York City–based bartender Hugo Ensslin's *Recipes for Mixed Drinks*, published in 1917. The drink was then lost for decades: It fell out of fashion, and then crème de violette, the ingredient that gives the cocktail its signature hue and floral flavor, became unavailable in the States by the 1960s.

One brand returned the violet liqueur Stateside in the mid-aughts and others soon followed. The Aviation regained its wings, and it now soars through the bars of NYC—and elsewhere—once again.

Aviation

Add all the ingredients to a cocktail shaker with ice and shake until well-chilled. Strain into a coupe glass. Garnish with a cocktail cherry and a lemon twist.

2 oz (60 ml) gin

¼ oz (10 ml) crème de violette

½ oz (15 ml) maraschino liqueur (preferably Luxardo)

¾ oz (20 ml) lemon juice, freshly squeezed

GARNISH

Cocktail cherry and lemon twist

At its simplest, the Gibson is essentially a Martini, distinguished by a pickled onion garnish. Several people have laid claim to this cocktail over the years, but the most frequently repeated origin story is that illustrator Charles Dana Gibson, the creator of the iconic Gibson Girl, challenged a bartender at The Players club in New York City to improve upon a standard Martini.

As with many classics, variations exist. The version Meaghan Dorman serves at her Dear Irving bars (one of which is just around the corner from The Players club) has become a city favorite. It uses sweet blanc vermouth rather than the dry version employed in most Martinis; the blanc's sweetness countering the savory umami flavors of the pickled cocktail onion. Dorman uses house-made pickled onions, but no one will judge if you use store-bought instead.

Gibson

Add all the ingredients to a mixing glass with ice and stir until well-chilled. Strain into a coupe glass. Garnish with two skewered pickled onions.

2 oz (60 ml) gin (preferably Tanqueray 10)

1 oz (30 ml) blanc vermouth (preferably Carpano bianco)

2 barspoons pickled onion brine (see page 161)

GARNISH

Pickled Onions (see page 161)

Locally sourced
Small batch GIN.
45%
700 ml
ARTISAN
Distilleries
GIN
MADE IN

This drink and the men's formal evening attire both take their name from the Tuxedo Club, a posh country club about an hour's drive from New York City.

The drink has undergone a few different incarnations since it was created around the turn of the previous century, the second of which—essentially a Martini with a bit of absinthe and maraschino liqueur added—has proved most popular over the decades. It makes an elegant evening sipper, no matter what you're wearing.

Tuxedo #2

¼ oz (10 ml) absinthe

2¼ oz (70 ml) gin (preferably Plymouth)

½ oz (15 ml) blanc vermouth (preferably Dolin blanc)

¼ oz (10 ml) maraschino liqueur (preferably Luxardo)

4 dashes orange bitters

GARNISH

Lemon or orange twist and cocktail cherry (optional)

Add the absinthe to a coupe or martini glass and swirl to coat the inside of the glass with the absinthe. Discard any extra.

Add the remaining ingredients to a mixing glass with ice and stir until well-chilled. Strain into the prepared glass. Garnish with a lemon or orange twist, and a cocktail cherry, if desired.

LUXARDO
The Original
MARASCHINO
Cherries
Ideal for cocktails
Made in Italy

CHAMPAGNE
Veuve Clicquot
MAISON FONDÉE EN 1772
BRUT
A REIMS-FRANCE

The French 75 may have originated elsewhere, most likely at the American Bar in Paris, but New Yorkers soon adopted the Champagne-heavy cocktail and have made it their own.

You might say it's because many of the city's residents embrace day-drinking as part of a glamorous weekend brunch at spots like Balthazar, and French 75s fit the bill perfectly, fueling gossipy dishings on the previous night's party exploits.

French 75

Add the gin, lemon juice, and syrup to a cocktail shaker with ice and shake until well-chilled. Strain into a flute glass. Top with Champagne and stir gently and briefly to combine. Garnish with a lemon twist, if desired.

1 oz (30 ml) gin

½ oz (15 ml) lemon juice, freshly squeezed

¼ oz (10 ml) Simple Syrup (see page 163)

3 oz (90 ml) Champagne (or other sparkling wine)

GARNISH

Lemon twist (optional)

Created in the early 1900s and one of the most popular cocktails of its day, this drink is believed to have been first shaken up at The Waldorf-Astoria, where it became the lunchtime special.

As the story goes, its creator named the drink for rowdy bar guests who brought to mind the animals he had encountered during a recent trip to the Bronx Zoo. A few of these cocktails in the early afternoon hours could make animals of us all.

Bronx

Add all the ingredients to a cocktail shaker with ice and shake until well-chilled. Strain into a coupe glass. Garnish with an orange twist, if desired.

- 2 oz (60 ml) gin
- ¼ oz (10 ml) dry vermouth
- ¼ oz (10 ml) sweet vermouth
- 1 oz (30 ml) orange juice, freshly squeezed
- 1 dash orange bitters (optional)

GARNISH

Orange twist (optional)

REGAN
Orange Bitt
№ 6

This refreshing summer cocktail is thought to have been created at the South Side Sportsmen's Club on Long Island for the club's well-heeled guests.

The original version called for both lemon and lime juice and a splash of soda; these days it generally loses both the fizz and lemon. You can certainly add a splash of soda water if you like, to harken back to *The Great Gatsby* times, but it's perfectly delicious without. Either way, it remains perfect for warm-weather country-club-style sipping.

Southside

Add the mint leaves and syrup to a cocktail shaker and gently muddle. Add the gin and lime juice, then add ice and shake until well-chilled. Strain into a coupe glass. Add a splash of soda water, if desired. Garnish with a mint sprig.

- 6–8 mint leaves
- ¾ oz (20 ml) Simple Syrup (see page 163)
- 2 oz (60 ml) gin
- ¾ oz (20 ml) lime juice, freshly squeezed
- Soda water, to top (optional)

GARNISH

Mint sprig

LIME

This is another cocktail that likely arose at The Waldorf-Astoria during the pre-Prohibition years and was, of course, created in honor of the comedic silent film star.

Note that this cocktail calls for sloe gin rather than the more common London dry style. Flavored with a fruit related to plums, this style of gin is rich and tart, imparting the lush, fruity notes essential to this drink.

Charlie Chaplin

Add all the ingredients to a cocktail shaker with ice and shake until well-chilled. Strain into a coupe or martini glass.

- 1 oz (30 ml) sloe gin
- 1 oz (30 ml) apricot brandy or liqueur (such as Rothman & Winter)
- 1 oz (30 ml) lime juice, freshly squeezed

Bearing hints of both a Manhattan (page 16) and a Bijou (page 27), this cocktail is all about big, bold flavors. It's said to have been created when a patron entered a bar humming "It's a Long Way to Tipperary" before requesting a drink.

Its recipe first appeared in Hugo Ensslin's 1917 cocktail book but, as with the Weeper's Joy (page 40), the folks at The Dead Rabbit have updated it for modern tastes, allowing the Irish whiskey to take the lead and adding dashes of other flavors for balance and complexity.

Tipperary

Add all the ingredients to a mixing glass with ice and stir until well-chilled. Strain into a Nick & Nora glass. Express the oils from an orange twist over the drink and discard the twist.

- 1½ oz (45 ml) Irish whiskey (preferably Powers John's Lane)
- 1½ oz (45 ml) sweet vermouth
- ½ oz (15 ml) green Chartreuse
- 2 dashes absinthe
- 2 dashes Angostura bitters
- 2 dashes orange bitters

GARNISH

Orange twist

F
Classic
Blend
PRODUCT OF IRELAND
40%Alc/Vol
700ml

New Yorkers sometimes mock the state just across the Hudson, but it does produce good drinks, such as this one that arose around the turn of the previous century and is attributed to either a Jersey City bartender who went by the name of Jack Rose, or a notorious gambler of the same moniker.

The cocktail notably employs applejack or apple brandy—ideally 100-proof Laird's straight apple brandy. Laird's is produced in New Jersey and is the oldest licensed distiller in the country.

Jack Rose

Add all the ingredients to a cocktail shaker with ice and shake until well-chilled. Strain into a coupe or martini glass. Garnish with a lemon twist.

NOTE

High-quality grenadine is essential for this drink. It's easy to make your own, otherwise go for the best store-bought grenadine you can find.

2 oz (60 ml) apple brandy (preferably Laird's 100-proof straight apple brandy)

1 oz (30 ml) lemon juice, freshly squeezed

¾ oz (20 ml) Grenadine (see page 159)

GARNISH

Lemon twist

LAIRD'S
APPLE
A SMOOTH BL
Distillers since 1780
LAIRD&COMPANY
AMERICA'S OLDEST
FAMILY-RUN DISTILLERS
40% ALC./VOL (80 PROOF)
GRENADINE
SYRUP
Syrup Co
0% proof

CRÈME DE CACAO
LIQUEUR for Cocktails
100ml

The original gin-based Alexander cocktail arose in New York City around 1914, and was commissioned from a bartender by the name of Troy Alexander at Rector's, a popular seafood restaurant, to launch an ad campaign by a railway company.

It wasn't until about a decade later in London that bartenders began swapping out the gin in favor of brandy, giving rise to the now more common variation of the cocktail. Either version yields a rich and creamy drink-your-dessert cocktail.

(Brandy) Alexander

Add all the ingredients to a cocktail shaker with ice and shake until well-chilled. Strain into a coupe or martini glass. Garnish with freshly grated nutmeg.

- 1½ oz (45 ml) brandy (or gin, if preferred)
- 1 oz (30 ml) crème de cacao
- 1 oz (30 ml) heavy cream (double cream)

GARNISH

Grated nutmeg

NYC
Never Stopped
Drinking

1920–1940s

BLOODY MARY

ALGONQUIN

APEROL SPRITZ

IRISH COFFEE

MARY PICKFORD

BETWEEN THE SHEETS

GYPSY QUEEN

THANKS FOR VISITING!

A version of this drink was first created at Harry's New York Bar in Paris in the 1920s by Fernand "Pete" Petiot. In 1934, Petiot brought his drink to New York City when he was hired by John Astor to work in the King Cole Bar in the St. Regis hotel, where it became known as the Red Snapper.

That drink gave rise to uncountable variations that are now served at brunches all over New York City. Take a cue from those and experiment with different spirits (vodka, gin, and tequila all work well) and different spices or flavorings, and get as creative with the garnishes as your imagination desires.

Bloody Mary

Add all the ingredients to a cocktail shaker with ice and shake until well-chilled. Strain into an ice-filled Collins glass. Garnish with a celery stalk, parsley sprig, lemon wedge, and whichever pickled vegetables you prefer.

- 2 oz (60 ml) vodka
- 4 oz (120 ml) tomato juice, chilled
- ½ oz (15 ml) lemon juice, freshly squeezed
- 2 dashes hot sauce (such as Tabasco)
- 2 dashes worcestershire sauce
- 1 barspoon jarred grated horseradish (optional)
- 1 pinch ground black pepper
- 1 pinch salt or celery salt

GARNISH

Celery stalk, parsley sprig, lemon wedge and your favorite pickled vegetables

HOLBROOKS
WORCESTERSHIRE SAUCE
250ml
McILHENNY CO
TABASCO
BRAND
PEPPER SAUCE

The Algonquin Hotel, which stands on 44th Street just off Times Square, is where members of the Algonquin Round Table—including Dorothy Parker as well as other notable writers and actors of the day—met to exchange *bons mots* in the 1920s and '30s. This cocktail arose in the 1930s, and whether or not it was created at the iconic hotel, it's certainly named for it.

After imbibing a few of these, you and everyone around you will likely seem a little wittier as well.

Algonquin

Add all the ingredients to a cocktail shaker with ice and shake until well-chilled. Strain into a coupe glass. Garnish with a pineapple wedge and/or a cocktail cherry, if desired.

1½ oz (45 ml) rye whiskey

¾ oz (20 ml) dry vermouth

¾ oz (20 ml) pineapple juice

2 dashes Peychaud's bitters

GARNISH

Pineapple wedge and/or cocktail cherry (optional)

THE Algonquin
A
A
59 63

APEROL
APEROL
ORIGINAL RECIPE
APERITIVO
SINCE
1919
LIQUEUR
PADOVA-ITALIA
SODA
WATER
Prosecco

On any given summer afternoon, you'll see innumerable New Yorkers drinking spritzes al fresco at sidewalk tables outside fashionable restaurants. Originally created in the Veneto region of Italy during the post-war years, the Aperol Spritz has been a New York City favorite for years.

In-the-know drinkers sometimes swap in other liqueurs in place of the orange-colored and gently bitter classic option. The Italian amaro Cynar is a go-to for an extra-bitter twist, while elderflower-flavored St-Germain adds a floral sweetness.

Aperol Spritz

Add all the ingredients to a large wine glass or balloon glass filled with plenty of ice. Stir gently and briefly to combine. Garnish with an orange wheel or two, as desired.

2 oz (60 ml) Aperol

3 oz (90 ml) Prosecco (or other sparkling wine)

1 oz (30 ml) soda water

GARNISH

1–2 orange wheels

This drink was created in an Irish airport bar in the 1940s. It may have visited San Francisco next, at the Buena Vista café, but it was perfected in New York City. Legendary bartender Dale DeGroff spent years reworking and perfecting the recipe for The Dead Rabbit, where it's now the bar's signature serve.

Freshly whipped cream is essential to the drink. You can whip the cream by beating it with a whisk or a mixer, but the fun way is to shake it in a cocktail shaker until it's thick and frothy.

Irish Coffee

Add the whiskey and demerara syrup to an Irish coffee glass. Pour in the hot coffee, leaving about a half-inch (1 cm) at the top of the glass, and stir gently to combine. Top with the whipped cream and garnish with freshly grated nutmeg.

1 oz (30 ml) Irish whiskey (preferably Bushmills Original)

½ oz (15 ml) Demerara Syrup (see page 157)

3½ oz (100 ml) hot coffee, medium-to-dark roast, preferably made in a French press

2 oz (60 ml) heavy (double) cream, freshly whipped

GARNISH

Grated nutmeg

OPEN
PASTURES
Heavy Cream
PASTURES
Quality since 1852
Heavy Cream
16 Fl

This drink was created in Havana, Cuba, during Prohibition times by an American bartender named Eddie Woelke, in honor of its namesake, a star of Broadway and the silver screen who split her time between New York City and Hollywood.

Fun fact: Pickford was friends with (and a business partner of) screen star Charlie Chaplin, who has a namesake cocktail of his own (page 63), and is said to have traveled to Cuba with him.

Mary Pickford

Add all the ingredients to a cocktail shaker with ice and shake until well-chilled. Strain into a cocktail or coupe glass. Garnish with a cocktail cherry, if desired.

1½ oz (45 ml) light rum

1 barspoon maraschino liqueur

1½ oz (45 ml) pineapple juice

¼ oz (10 ml) Grenadine (see page 159)

GARNISH

Cocktail cherry (optional)

PREMIUM
Liqueurs
TRIPLE
SEC

Harry MacElhone of Harry's New York Bar in Paris often gets credited with creating this cocktail, but contemporary theories suggest the drink originated in New York City during early Prohibition times as a gin-and-rum-based drink, which then traveled to Paris, where the gin was swapped out in favor of brandy.

In any case, it made its way back Stateside by 1934, by which point it was included in *The Official Mixer's Manual* by Patrick Gavin Duffy, the longtime head bartender at the former Ashland House Hotel in NYC.

Between the Sheets

Add all the ingredients to a cocktail shaker with ice and shake until well-chilled. Strain into a coupe glass. Garnish with an orange twist.

1 oz (30 ml) Cognac

1 oz (30 ml) light rum

1 oz (30 ml) triple sec

½ oz (15 ml) lemon juice, freshly squeezed

GARNISH

Orange twist

The Gypsy Queen, believed to be among the first vodka cocktails created in the United States, originated at the Russian Tea Room in the years immediately following the repeal of Prohibition.

That restaurant, founded during the Prohibition years by former members of the Russian Imperial Ballet, remains a popular destination for imbibing vodka—and caviar, and more—in opulent Art Deco surroundings just south of Central Park.

Gypsy Queen

Add all the ingredients to a mixing glass with ice and stir until well-chilled. Strain into a Nick & Nora glass. Garnish with a lemon or orange twist, as desired.

2 oz (60 ml) vodka

1 oz (30 ml) Bénédictine

1 dash Angostura bitters

GARNISH

Lemon or orange twist

D.O.M
D.O.M
Le Directeur
BÉNÉDICTINE
Liqueur

Modern Classics

1980–2010

See you next time!

COSMOPOLITAN

GOLD RUSH

NAKED & FAMOUS

FITZGERALD

TRINIDAD SOUR

RITZ COCKTAIL

PENICILLIN

ESPRESSO MARTINI

OLD CUBAN

GIN-GIN MULE

OAXACA OLD FASHIONED

SIESTA

HAITIAN DIVORCE

BENSONHURST

GIN BLOSSOM

NEW YORK CITY, USA

Before the Cosmopolitan was Carrie Bradshaw's cocktail of choice on *Sex and the City*, it was Madonna's favorite drink at the Odeon, the downtown hotspot where the cocktail was created by bartender Toby Cecchini in the late 1980s.

The Cosmo is experiencing a resurgence on drink menus all over New York City, as a fresh crop of drinkers realize how delicious it is. Just be sure to use citron vodka instead of the unflavored stuff to add an essential boost of brightness.

Cosmopolitan

Add all the ingredients to a cocktail shaker with ice and shake until well-chilled. Strain into a martini glass. Garnish with a lemon twist.

1½ oz (45 ml) citron vodka (such as Absolut Citron)

¾ oz (20 ml) Cointreau

¾ oz (20 ml) lime juice, freshly squeezed

¾ oz (20 ml) cranberry juice

GARNISH

Lemon twist

W BROADWAY
CAFETERIA
ONE WAY
ONE WAY
ODEON
BRASSERIE

The pioneering bar Milk & Honey, opened in January 2000 by Sasha Petraske, did more than perhaps any other cocktail bar to usher in the contemporary cocktail renaissance. (The bar is now closed, but its space lives on as Attaboy, helmed by some of the same team.)

Petraske and T.J. Siegal created this riff on a classic whiskey sour in 2000, replacing the usual sugar-based simple syrup with a rich honey syrup. It's a shining example of the style of drinks created at the bar: a minimalist three-ingredient cocktail with proportions dialed in to perfection.

Gold Rush

Add all the ingredients to a cocktail shaker with ice and shake until well-chilled. Strain into a rocks glass over a large ice cube. Garnish with a lemon twist, if desired.

- 2 oz (60 ml) bourbon
- ¾ oz (20 ml) lemon juice, freshly squeezed
- ¾ oz (20 ml) Rich Honey Syrup (see page 162)

GARNISH

Lemon twist (optional)

BOURBON
SMALL BATCH
AGED IN
AMERICAN OAK

ARTESANAL
MEZCAL
OAXACA
100% AGAVE
WITH AGAVE WORM

This complex yet refreshing cocktail has proven to be the most popular creation by Joaquín Simó, who first shook up this modern classic in 2011 while at Death & Co. Inspired by both the classic Last Word and the modern-classic Paper Plane, this drink employs the equal-parts formula common to both cocktails, but swaps in some bold and unexpected flavors.

Naked & Famous

Add all the ingredients to a cocktail shaker and shake until well-chilled. Strain into a coupe glass.

- ¾ oz (20 ml) mezcal (ideally Del Maguey Chichicapa)
- ¾ oz (20 ml) Aperol
- ¾ oz (20 ml) yellow Chartreuse
- ¾ oz (20 ml) lime juice, freshly squeezed

This cocktail is named for the writer who chronicled the Jazz Age so memorably in *The Great Gatsby* and other works. It would be easy to assume it's a pre-Prohibition-era classic, but it is in fact a much more recent creation: The drink was first shaken in the 1990s by Dale DeGroff during his tenure at the Rainbow Room. It goes just as well with jazz as do cocktails created a century earlier.

Fitzgerald

Add all the ingredients to a cocktail shaker with ice and shake until well-chilled. Strain into a rocks glass over ice. Garnish with a lemon wheel.

1½ oz (45 ml) gin

¾ oz (20 ml) lemon juice, freshly squeezed

¾ oz (20 ml) Simple Syrup (see page 163)

2 dashes Angostura bitters

GARNISH

Lemon wheel

BOMBAY
SAPPHIRE
Distilled
LONDON
DRY GIN

Bartender Giuseppe González initially raised a lot of eyebrows with this unusual cocktail, which he created for a competition while working at Clover Club and which has since spread far and wide. The drink is notable for featuring Angostura bitters, a substance usually measured in dashes, not ounces, as its base.

The Angostura's clove-heavy baking-spice flavors are brightened with lemon juice and tamed with rich orgeat (a sweet syrup typically made from almonds and sugar), but it's still a beast of a drink. It's a love-it-or-hate-it cocktail and perhaps an acquired taste, but, well, so is New York City.

Trinidad Sour

Add all the ingredients to a cocktail shaker with ice and shake until well-chilled. Strain into a Nick & Nora or coupe glass.

- 1½ oz (45 ml) Angostura bitters
- ½ oz (15 ml) rye whiskey (preferably 100-proof)
- ¾ oz (20 ml) lemon juice, freshly squeezed
- 1 oz (30 ml) orgeat

The Best
Est 1999
SYRUP CO
BARTENDER
ORGEAT
SYRUP
ANGOSTURA
200 ml
Barrel
SINGLE BARREL
100 Proof
STRAIGHT RYE
WHISKY

Dale DeGroff has earned the nickname "King Cocktail" and is the person who, more than any other, is responsible for the contemporary cocktail renaissance. While bartending at the Rainbow Room in the late 1980s through the '90s, he resurrected many classic cocktails and the use of fresh ingredients, and devised many cocktails of his own.

When asked which drink he would choose to represent his legacy, he named his Ritz Cocktail, which he created in 1985 while at the NYC restaurant Aurora, where he did "research" in advance of his time at the Rainbow Room. "It's never a bad time for a Champagne cocktail," says DeGroff.

Ritz Cocktail

1 oz (30 ml) Cognac (preferably Courvoisier VSOP)

½ oz (15 ml) Cointreau

¼ oz (10 ml) maraschino liqueur (preferably Luxardo)

¼ oz (10 ml) lemon juice, freshly squeezed

2 oz (60 ml) Champagne, chilled

GARNISH

Orange zest "coin", about the size of a quarter (1 in/2.5 cm)

Add the Cognac, Cointreau, maraschino liqueur, and lemon juice to a cocktail shaker with ice and shake until well-chilled. Strain into a coupe glass. Top with the Champagne.

Hold the piece of orange zest over the drink, skin side down. Light a match and use it to warm the zest. Squeeze the zest toward the flame and the surface of the drink; the oils will briefly spark, caramelizing their flavors.

Discard the zest or drop it into the drink to garnish.

The Penicillin is another drink to emerge from Milk & Honey that has found its way into bars around the globe. Bartender Sam Ross was playing with variations on the Gold Rush (page 90)—which, by 2005, was already considered a modern classic—and came up with this now iconic cocktail. A little smoky, a little spicy, it's just what the doctor ordered.

Penicillin

- 2 oz (60 ml) blended Scotch whisky
- ¾ oz (20 ml) lemon juice, freshly squeezed
- ½ oz (15 ml) Ginger Syrup (see page 158)
- ½ oz (15 ml) Rich Honey Syrup (see page 162)
- ¼ oz (10 ml) peated (Islay) Scotch whisky

GARNISH

Candied ginger

Add the blended whisky, lemon juice, ginger syrup, and honey syrup to a cocktail shaker with ice and shake until well-chilled. Strain into a rocks glass over one large ice cube.

Place a spoon over the glass, facing downward, with the tip just touching the liquid, and slowly pour the peated whisky on top of the drink over the back of the spoon so that it floats on top of the liquid. Garnish with a piece of candied ginger.

The Espresso Martini was originally created in London in the 1980s by bartender Dick Bradsell, but in recent years it has become New York City's unofficial signature drink. After all, *something* has to fuel "the city that never sleeps".

There are endless renditions of the cocktail around town, but you can't go wrong with this most classic version.

Espresso Martini

Add all the ingredients to a cocktail shaker with ice and shake until well-chilled. Strain into a coupe or martini glass. Garnish with three coffee beans.

2 oz (60 ml) vodka

½ oz (15 ml) coffee liqueur (preferably Mr. Black)

1 oz (30 ml) espresso, brewed and cooled, or cold-brew concentrate

GARNISH

3 coffee beans

7
EL RON DE CUBA
Havana
Club
MADE AND AGED IN CUBA
AÑEJO 7 AÑO7

This elevated homage to the Mojito was created by Audrey Saunders, a protégée of Dale DeGroff. The drink made its first appearance in 2002 at Bemelmans Bar at The Carlyle, where Saunders was then working. It has traveled the world in the meantime, and remains on the menu at Bemelmans, a perennial hotspot for the see-and-be-seen set.

Old Cuban

Add the lime juice, simple syrup, and mint leaves to a cocktail shaker and gently muddle. Add the rum and bitters with ice, and shake until well-chilled. Strain into a coupe glass. Top with the Champagne. Garnish with a mint sprig and a lime wheel.

- ¾ oz (20 ml) lime juice, freshly squeezed
- 1 oz (30 ml) Simple Syrup (see page 163)
- 6–8 mint leaves
- 1½ oz (45 ml) aged rum
- 2 dashes Angostura bitters
- 2 oz (60 ml) Champagne

GARNISH

Mint sprig and lime wheel

Audrey Saunders went on to open Pegu Club with Julie Reiner in 2005, which was then among the first cocktail bars of the contemporary resurgence in New York. This cocktail, like her Old Cuban (page 105), shares many characteristics with a Mojito and also borrows a bit from the Moscow Mule. It became a house favorite at Pegu Club and elsewhere.

Gin-Gin Mule

¾ oz (20 ml) lime juice, freshly squeezed

1 oz (30 ml) Simple Syrup (see page 163)

1 mint sprig

1¾ oz (50 ml) gin (preferably Tanqueray)

1 oz (30 ml) Ginger Beer (see page 158 or use store-bought; see Note)

GARNISH

Mint sprig, lime wheel and/or candied ginger (optional)

Add the lime juice, simple syrup, and mint sprig to a cocktail shaker and gently muddle. Add the gin and ginger beer (if using homemade). Add ice and shake until well-chilled. Strain into a highball glass over ice.

Top with ginger beer (if using store-bought) and stir gently and briefly to combine.

Garnish with a mint sprig, plus a lime wheel and/or piece of candied ginger, if desired. Serve with a straw.

NOTE

Saunders' recipe calls for a house-made ginger beer. If you're pressed for time, store-bought is fine, but be sure to use ginger beer, not ginger ale, for its more intense flavor. The homemade ginger beer won't be fizzy and can be shaken with the other ingredients. If you go with store-bought, add it afterward.

LONDON DRY
GIN
IMPORTED
700 mls
40% Vol
GINGER
Beer
330 mls
0% ABV

It sounds like such a simple idea: Make an Old Fashioned (page 21), but swap in tequila and a touch of mezcal in place of the usual whiskey. But in 2007, the year this drink was first stirred at the East Village cocktail bar Death & Co by Phil Ward, mezcal was a fairly new addition to the spirits scene and not yet used in many cocktails.

Since then, this spirit-forward sipper has become the most requested drink ever created at Death & Co, and it now appears on bar menus around the world.

Oaxaca Old Fashioned

Add all the ingredients to a mixing glass with ice and stir until well-chilled. Strain into a rocks glass over one large ice cube.

Hold the piece of orange zest over the drink, skin side down. Light a match and use it to warm the zest. Squeeze the zest toward the flame and the surface of the drink; the oils will briefly spark, caramelizing their flavors.

Discard the zest or drop it into the drink to garnish.

1½ oz (45 ml) reposado tequila (preferably El Tesoro)

½ oz (15 ml) mezcal (preferably Del Maguey San Luis Del Rio)

1 barspoon agave nectar

2 dashes Angostura bitters

GARNISH

Orange zest "coin", about the size of a quarter (1 in/2.5 cm)

CAM
TEQU
100% AGAV

Katie Stipe created this cocktail in 2006 while working at Flatiron Lounge under Julie Reiner. It's a tequila-based twist on a Hemingway Daiquiri (said to be the famed writer's drink of choice in Havana), and functions as a great gateway to Campari and other aperitivi and amari. The drink's tart, bright, and gently bitter flavors will perk you up just as well as an afternoon nap.

Siesta

Add all the ingredients to a cocktail shaker with ice and shake until well-chilled. Strain into a coupe glass. Garnish with a lime wheel.

- 1½ oz (45 ml) blanco tequila
- ¼ oz (10 ml) Campari
- ¾ oz (20 ml) lime juice, freshly squeezed
- ½ oz (15 ml) grapefruit juice, freshly squeezed
- ¾ oz (20 ml) Simple Syrup (see page 163)

GARNISH

Lime wheel

Drinks pro Tom Richter created the Haitian Divorce in 2012 while at The Beagle in New York City. It's essentially a riff on an Old Fashioned (page 21), employing both rum and mezcal, which together with their respective earthiness and smoke evoke the flavor of Scotch whisky.

Rather than a divorce, this cocktail is a lovely marriage of two spirits that don't appear together in a drink often enough.

Haitian Divorce

Add all the ingredients to a mixing glass with ice and stir until well-chilled. Strain into a rocks glass over one large ice cube. Express the oils from an orange twist and a lime twist over the drink, then drop both twists into the glass to garnish.

1½ oz (45 ml) aged rum (preferably Barbancourt 8)

¾ oz (20 ml) mezcal espadin

½ oz (15 ml) Pedro Ximénez sherry (preferably Lustau)

2 dashes Angostura bitters

GARNISH

Orange and lime twists

Rhum
Barbancourt
HAITIEN DEPUIS 1862
VIEILLI 4 ANS
AGED 4 YEARS
HAITI

At Milk & Honey, bartenders created a variety of riffs on the classic Brooklyn cocktail (page 48), naming each after a different Brooklyn neighborhood.

The Bensonhurst, created by Chad Solomon in 2006, is among the most popular of the resulting creations and arguably the most delicious. Named for the south Brooklyn neighborhood that was traditionally home to an Italian population, the Bensonhurst swaps in the Italian amaro Cynar in place of Amer Picon and retains the Italian maraschino liqueur, making for a deliciously bitter and Italian-inflected version of the classic cocktail.

Bensonhurst

Combine all the ingredients in a mixing glass with ice and stir until well-chilled. Strain into a coupe glass.

- 2 oz (60 ml) rye whiskey (preferably Rittenhouse)
- 1 oz (30 ml) dry vermouth (preferably Dolin)
- 2 barspoons maraschino liqueur (preferably Luxardo)
- 1 heavy (generous) barspoon Cynar

CYNAR
RICETTA ORIGINALE

CLOVER CLUB
NY
210

Julie Reiner created this Martini variation for the opening of Clover Club in 2008, and it hasn't left the bar's menu since, also appearing on bar menus worldwide in the meantime.

This Martini's appeal is in the details. Rather than the more common London dry, Reiner reaches for Plymouth gin—both a brand and a separate style, softer and more citrus-forward. She also employs blanc vermouth, the sweeter cousin of the dry style generally used in Martinis. With a touch of apricot eau de vie contributing further complexity, it all adds up to a fruity, floral, aromatic, and elegant sipper.

Gin Blossom

Add all the ingredients to a mixing glass with ice and stir until well-chilled. Strain into a coupe glass. Express the oils from an orange twist over the drink, then drop the twist into the glass to garnish.

1½ oz (45 ml) Plymouth gin

1½ oz (45 ml) blanc vermouth (such as Martini & Rossi Bianco)

¾ oz (20 ml) apricot eau de vie

2 dashes orange bitters

GARNISH

Orange twist

Contemporary Creations

2011–Present

LOVE & MURDER

A ROSE AMONG THORNS

MERMAID PARADE

OH MY WORD!

DEACON BLUES

DEBBIE, DON'T

MEZCAL MULE

PSYCHO KILLER

YELLOW JACKET

SPEAK LOW

MIDNIGHT MARAUDER

WILDEST REDHEAD

TIA MIA

ABSINTHE COLADA

LEFT HAND

GUILLOTINE

DIRTY DOG MARTINI

RECEIPT NO. 950131

Campari and green Chartreuse are two of the most intensely flavored liqueurs in the drinks world—and two of the most polarizing as well. This cocktail, created by Nick Bennett during his time as the bar director at Porchlight, employs both in what's essentially a riff on a standard sour, but is anything but ordinary. The drink became an instant favorite at the bar and hasn't been off the menu since.

Love & Murder

Add all the ingredients to a cocktail shaker with ice and shake until well-chilled. Strain into a coupe glass.

- 1 oz (30 ml) Campari
- 1 oz (30 ml) green Chartreuse
- 1 oz (30 ml) lime juice, freshly squeezed
- ¾ oz (20 ml) Simple Syrup (see page 163)
- 4 drops Saline Solution (see page 163)

CHART
1605

The Up & Up, the cocktail bar where owner Matt Piacentini created this cocktail, is housed in a storied space in Greenwich Village and in the city's history, occupying what was once the Gaslight Café, the famed beatnik hangout of the 1960s.

The first cocktail created for the bar, this Martini variation from the bar's very first menu in 2015 remains popular among Up & Up's loyal regulars.

A Rose Among Thorns

Add all the ingredients to a mixing glass with ice and stir until well-chilled. Strain into a coupe glass. Express the oils from a lemon twist over the drink, then drop the twist into the glass to garnish.

1 oz (30 ml) Roku gin

1 oz (30 ml) aquavit (such as Brennivin or Krogstad)

½ oz (15 ml) Amaro Montenegro

½ oz (15 ml) Dolin dry vermouth

2 dashes orange bitters

GARNISH

Lemon twist

116
UP & UP
COCKTAILS
Downstairs

JLP
JEAN-LUC PASQUET
Marie-Framboise
APÉRITIF À BASE DE COGNAC & FRAMBOISE
75 mls
PRODUCT OF FRANCE
16% alc/Vol
EDIBLE SPARKLES
RAINBOW

The Mermaid Parade is held along the Coney Island boardwalk each June, a celebration of sea creatures and the summer solstice. Said to be the nation's largest art parade, it involves bright colors, frothy costumes, and copious amounts of glitter—as does this cocktail, which was created by Natasha David at the now-shuttered bar Nitecap. Festive and fruity, this low-alcohol cocktail is the ideal accompaniment to summer merriment.

Mermaid Parade

Add all the ingredients, except the soda water, to a cocktail shaker without ice. Shake vigorously until frothy (about 20 seconds). Open the shaker and add ice, and vigorously shake again until well-chilled. Strain into a Collins glass.

Slowly and gently add an ounce or two (30–60 ml) of soda water, so the frothy top rises just above the rim of the glass. Sprinkle with edible glitter, if desired.

1½ oz (45 ml) Aperol

¾ oz (20 ml) Pasquet Marie-Framboise

¾ oz (20 ml) grapefruit juice, freshly squeezed

½ oz (15 ml) lemon juice, freshly squeezed

½ oz (15 ml) Simple Syrup (see page 163)

1 egg white

Soda water, to top

GARNISH

Edible glitter (optional)

The East Village bar Amor y Amargo is renowned for its focus on bitters and bitter liqueurs. This drink—created by the bar's proprietor, Sother Teague, as a riff on the pre-Prohibition classic the Last Word—is a shining example of AyA's dogmatic stirred-only approach to cocktails: It echoes the flavors of that classic, while replacing its lime juice with lime bitters and a bright, juicy amaro, resulting in a silky, spirit-forward sipper.

Oh My Word!

Add all the ingredients to a mixing glass with ice and stir until well-chilled. Strain into a rocks glass or coupe glass. If desired, express the oils from a lemon twist over the drink, then garnish with the twist.

1 oz (30 ml) Old Tom gin (preferably Hayman's)

1 oz (30 ml) Amaro Montenegro

½ oz (15 ml) green Chartreuse

½ oz (15 ml) maraschino liqueur (preferably Luxardo)

4 dashes lime bitters (preferably Scrappy's)

GARNISH

Lemon twist (optional)

LIME
HANDCRAFTED BY
SCRAPPY
LIME
BITTERS
LUXARDO
LIQUEUR
GIROLAMO LUXARDO
IN TORREGLIA
CHARTREUS
AMARO
MONTENEGO
PREMIATA 1885 SPECIALITA
AMOR Y AMARGO

The Deacon Blues is a spin on the Old Fashioned (page 21) created by Sarah Morrissey at Dear Irving, an elegant cocktail bar near New York City's posh Gramercy Park.

Sure, the drink is named for the Steely Dan tune (the band hails from a town a few hours up the Hudson River from NYC), but instead of the Scotch whisky cited in the song's chorus, this cocktail's base is a combination of bourbon and mezcal, with other ingredients adding notes of vanilla, black pepper and baking spices. It's a comforting wintertime variation on that most classic of cocktails.

Deacon Blues

Add all the ingredients to a mixing glass with ice and stir until well-chilled. Strain into a rocks glass over one large ice cube. Garnish with a lime twist, and black pepper, if desired.

- 1½ oz (45 ml) 100-proof bourbon (preferably Old Forester)
- ½ oz (15 ml) mezcal (preferably Agave de Cortes)
- ¼ oz (10 ml) Black Pepper Vanilla Syrup (see page 156)
- 2 dashes Angostura bitters

GARNISH

Lime twist and cracked black pepper (optional)

PURE CANADIAN
MAPLE SYUP
100% NATURAL
250mL
1868
AMARO
AVERNA
ICILIANO

This cocktail was created by Zachary Gelnaw-Rubin while bartending at Dutch Kills in Long Island City, Queens, and is named for the ghost who's said to haunt the bar—or, more specifically, the usual verbal response of the bar staff to the ghost's antics.

Some bartenders take the drink's autumnal flavors a step further by using aged rum in place of the reposado tequila. Whichever way you enjoy it, it's a drink that's sure to lift your spirits—or summon them.

Debbie, Don't

Add all the ingredients to a cocktail shaker with ice and shake until well-chilled. Strain into a coupe glass.

- 1 oz (30 ml) tequila reposado
- 1 oz (30 ml) Amaro Averna
- ¾ oz (20 ml) lemon juice, freshly squeezed
- ½ oz (15 ml) maple syrup

PDT, on St. Mark's Place in the East Village, was among the city's first speakeasy-style spots when it opened in 2007. The bar is accessed via a phone booth in a hot-dog stand, an entry that continues to delight visitors to the bar.

A mule-style cocktail, in its simplest form, adds lime and ginger to its base spirit. This one, created in 2008 at PDT by Jim Meehan, expands that formula, adding a whole host of traditional Oaxacan flavors to the mix.

Mezcal Mule

Add the cucumber slices and agave nectar to a cocktail shaker and muddle. Add the mezcal, lime juice, and passionfruit purée. Add ice and shake until well-chilled. Strain into a large rocks glass over ice. Top with the ginger beer.

Garnish with a slice of cucumber and a piece of candied ginger. Sprinkle chili powder over the drink.

- 3 cucumber slices
- ½ oz (15 ml) agave nectar
- 1½ oz (45 ml) mezcal
- ¾ oz (20 ml) lime juice, freshly squeezed
- ¾ oz (20 ml) passionfruit purée (preferably Boiron)
- 1 oz (30 ml) Ginger Beer (see page 158 or use store-bought)

GARNISH

Cucumber slice, candied ginger and chili powder

SERVE CHILLED
BOTANICALLY
BREWED
CLASSIC
GINGER
BEE

Jillian Vose, the longtime beverage director at The Dead Rabbit, created this cocktail for one of the bar's earliest menus, and it has become one of its signature drinks. The cocktail, of course, shares its name with a song by Talking Heads, one of the greatest bands to ever come out of New York City.

The Dead Rabbit focuses on Irish whiskey, and the banana and chocolate liqueurs used in this cocktail were chosen, says Vose, to enhance the "Christmas-cake qualities" of the particular whiskey this cocktail employs.

Psycho Killer

- 2 oz (60 ml) Irish whiskey (preferably Redbreast 12 Single Pot Still)
- ¾ oz (20 ml) Campari
- ½ oz (15 ml) Giffard Banane du Brésil
- ½ oz (15 ml) white crème de cacao (such as Giffard)
- 2 dashes absinthe (preferably Vieux Pontarlier)

Add all the ingredients to a mixing glass with ice and stir until well-chilled. Strain into a Nick & Nora glass.

The Dead Rabbit
The Dead Rabbit

1795
TEQUILA
BLUE AGAVE
Alc Vol 43% 750mls

Those wandering in the West Village often wonder about the fortune teller in the window on Hudson Street. Behind the seer's lair lies a cocktail bar: Employees Only.

This cocktail, created at EO and named for the wasps that inhabit tequila distilleries and agave farms, is round and lush. There's quite a bit of booze in the glass, however, so too many of these will sting as badly as the drink's namesake.

Yellow Jacket

Add all the ingredients to a mixing glass with ice and stir until well-chilled. Strain into a coupe glass. Garnish with a lemon twist.

2 oz (60 ml) tequila (preferably Partida reposado)

1 oz (30 ml) St-Germain elderflower liqueur

¾ oz (20 ml) yellow Chartreuse

1 dash orange bitters (preferably Regans')

GARNISH

Lemon twist

Matcha, the powdered green tea, is currently having a big moment in New York City, but this cocktail predates that trend by many years. Pioneering bar Angel's Share, where the cocktail was created, itself predated the contemporary cocktail renaissance: It launched in 1993 and is said to have directly influenced Sasha Petraske, who opened his trailblazing Milk & Honey in 2000.

This drink, created in 2012 by Shingo Gokan for a prestigious cocktail competition—which he won—has remained on the Angel's Share bar menu ever since. Bright yet rich, sweet yet earthy, it's as soothing as the Japanese tea-making ritual its preparation evokes.

Speak Low

Add the rum and matcha powder to a small ceramic bowl. Use a chasen (bamboo whisk) to whisk them together until combined and slightly frothy.

Transfer the mixture to a cocktail shaker and add the sherry. Add ice and shake until well-chilled. Strain into a rocks glass over one large ice cube. Zest some yuzu or grapefruit peel over the top.

2 oz (60 ml) Bacardi Reserva Ocho rum

1 teaspoon matcha powder

½ oz (15 ml) Pedro Ximénez sherry

GARNISH

Yuzu zest (or grapefruit zest)

OCHO
BACARDÍ
GRAN RESERVE
RON
AGED
VIEILLI
8
AÑOS
YEARS
ANS

It's perhaps not as well known as his Naked & Famous (page 92), but this drink from Joaquín Simó has become a favorite among in-the-know drinkers. Taking the same format as a classic Negroni, this drink replaces the usual ingredients with ones that evoke the rich, smoky, spiced flavors of Oaxaca. The resulting sipper is lush and velvety, making for an ideal nightcap.

Midnight Marauder

- 1 oz (30 ml) mezcal (preferably Del Maguey Vida)
- 1 oz (30 ml) Bonal (a French aperitif)
- 1 oz (30 ml) Cynar
- 1 dash Bittermens Xocolatl Mole Bitters

Add all the ingredients to a mixing glass with ice and stir until well-chilled. Strain into a coupe or Nick & Nora glass.

VIDA
MEZCAL
Clásico
BONA
GENTIANE QUINA
APÉRITIF
des Montagnes
INVENTÉ
BONAL
A St. LAURENT-DU-PO

“A whiskey sour with a hug” is how Meaghan Dorman, this cocktail’s creator and the bar director at the Raines Law Room and Dear Irving, describes her drink. Honey and lemon provide familiar soothing flavors, while the allspice dram’s baking-spice elements lend a wintertime touch.

The drink gets drizzled with cherry liqueur before serving. You can expect it to sink to the bottom of the glass, bringing to mind an inverted New York Sour.

Wildest Redhead

Add the whisky, allspice dram, lemon juice, and honey syrup to a cocktail shaker with ice and shake until well-chilled. Strain into a rocks glass filled with ice. Drizzle the cherry liqueur over the top of the drink.

- 1½ oz (45 ml) blended Scotch whisky
- ¼ oz (10 ml) allspice dram liqueur
- ¾ oz (20 ml) lemon juice, freshly squeezed
- ½ oz (15 ml) Rich Honey Syrup (see page 162)
- ¼ oz (10 ml) Heering cherry liqueur

Bartender Ivy Mix created this cocktail at the tiki bar Lani Kai, and it later rose to fame at her Brooklyn bar Leyenda, which focused on Latin American spirits and flavors.

A take on the classic Mai Tai (the name gives it away), this version adds mezcal to the usual mix, lending an added dimension and helping to counteract the classic tiki drink's typical sweetness.

Tia Mia

Add all the ingredients to a cocktail shaker with ice and shake until well-chilled. Strain into a large rocks glass filled with pebble ice. Garnish with a lime wheel, a mint sprig, and an edible orchid. Serve with a straw.

1 oz (30 ml) mezcal (preferably Del Maguey Vida)

1 oz (30 ml) Jamaican rum (preferably Appleton Estate Signature Blend)

½ oz (15 ml) orange curaçao

¾ oz (20 ml) lime juice, freshly squeezed

½ oz (15 ml) orgeat

GARNISH

Lime wheel, mint sprig and edible orchid

This festive drink, one of the signature cocktails of absinthe-focused Brooklyn bar Maison Premiere, successfully combines two wildly disparate flavors—those of the tropical Piña Colada and sophisticated, herbaceous absinthe—into one cooling and refreshing cocktail.

The icy mixture is a particularly welcome treat during the hot, humid days of a New York City summer. If you can't drink it in Maison Premiere's lush, verdant garden, making it at home is the next-best thing.

Absinthe Colada

Combine all the ingredients in a hurricane glass, then fill the glass three-quarters full with crushed or pebble ice. Swizzle with a swizzle stick for 10–15 seconds. Fill the glass the rest of the way with more crushed or pebble ice, mounding it slightly at the top. Garnish with a mint bouquet and serve with a straw.

- 1 oz (30 ml) absinthe
- ½ oz (15 ml) rhum agricole, such as Rhum J.M blanc
- 1 teaspoon crème de menthe
- 1 oz (30 ml) pineapple juice
- ½ oz (15 ml) lemon juice, freshly squeezed
- 1 oz (30 ml) Coconut Syrup (see page 156)

GARNISH

Mint bouquet

HANDCRAFTED
BOB'S BITTERS
SMALL BATCH
CHOCOLATE
ALL NATURAL COCOA

During the early days of seminal cocktail bar Milk & Honey, the team created a series of "Hand" cocktails. This one by Sam Ross was said to perhaps be the favorite of the bar's founder, Sasha Petraske, and is a spin on a Boulevardier, itself a classic riff on the Negroni.

The resulting cocktail lands somewhere between a Negroni and a Manhattan, with the bitters adding an earthy baking-spice note.

Bonus: If you use aged rum rather than bourbon, the resulting cocktail will be the one the team dubbed the Right Hand, an equally delicious drink.

Left Hand

Add all the ingredients to a mixing glass with ice and stir until well-chilled. Strain into a coupe glass. Garnish with a cocktail cherry.

- 1½ oz (45 ml) bourbon
- ¾ oz (20 ml) Campari
- ¾ oz (20 ml) sweet vermouth (preferably Carpano Antica)
- 3 dashes chocolate bitters

GARNISH

Cocktail cherry

Behind a bookshelf in Brooklyn restaurant Chez Moi lies the secret entrance to Marie Antoinette–inspired bar Le Boudoir, a subterranean room of wine-colored velvet and gilded mirrors. Its original bar manager, Franky Marshall, created this smoky, spirit-forward cocktail, the name a nod to the queen's end during the French Revolution.

The drink's name also provides an apt warning against having too many of these strong concoctions: You may just lose your head.

Guillotine

Add all the ingredients to a mixing glass with ice and stir until well-chilled. Strain into a large snifter over ice. Express the oils from a lemon twist over the drink, then drop the twist into the glass or discard.

1 oz (30 ml) mezcal

¾ oz (20 ml) blended Scotch whisky

¼ oz (10 ml) banana liqueur (preferably Giffard Crème de Banane)

¼ oz (10 ml) Honey Syrup (see page 159)

GARNISH

Lemon twist

Hot dogs sold from street carts—“dirty-water dogs” to locals—can be found on seemingly every street corner throughout Manhattan, and this Martini variation from the folks at Brooklyn bar Grand Army took its inspiration from that ubiquitous snack. It's a little savory, a touch sweet, and entirely perfect with just about any food—including hot dogs, as this writer will vouch. The full recipe does require a couple of extra steps (infusing vermouth and pickling cherry tomatoes), but you'll find it's worth it.

Dirty Dog Martini

Add all the ingredients to a mixing glass with ice and stir until well-chilled. Strain into a Nick & Nora glass. Garnish with a pickled cherry tomato on a pick.

- 1½ oz (45 ml) gin (Grand Army uses Neversink Spirits)
- ½ oz (15 ml) dill aquavit
- ½ oz (15 ml) “Dog Water” Vermouth (see page 157)
- ½ oz (15 ml) blanc vermouth (such as Dolin blanc)
- 2 dashes bay leaf bitters (such as Matchbook Distilling Co.)
- 1 dash Saline Solution (see page 163)

GARNISH

Pickled Cherry Tomato (see page 160)

DILL
ANGELICA
YARROW
NASTURTIUM
NORDEN AQUAVIT
EXCEPTIONALLY CRAFTED
TRADITIONAL BOTANICAL SPIRIT
NET CONT
750 ML
45% ALC
BY VOL
CORIANDER
LOVAGE
CALENDULA
FENNEL

Syrups, Infusions & Garnishes

TABLE 31.

BLACK PEPPER VANILLA SYRUP

COCONUT SYRUP

DEMERARA SYRUP

"DOG WATER" VERMOUTH

GINGER BEER

GINGER SYRUP

GRENADINE

HONEY SYRUP

PICKLED CHERRY TOMATOES

PICKLED ONIONS & BRINE

RASPBERRY SYRUP

RICH HONEY SYRUP

SALINE SOLUTION

SIMPLE SYRUP

THANK YOU FOR VISITING!

Black pepper vanilla syrup

Combine the ingredients in a small saucepan over medium–low heat and stir until the sugar has dissolved. Remove from the heat and allow to cool. Strain through a fine-mesh strainer, discarding the solids. The syrup will keep, tightly sealed and refrigerated, for up to 1 month.

1 cup (240 ml) water

1 cup (200 g) sugar

1 vanilla bean, split open

40 cracks fresh black pepper

Coconut syrup

Combine the ingredients in a saucepan over low heat and stir until well mixed. Remove from the heat and allow to cool. The syrup will keep, tightly sealed and refrigerated, for up to 1 month.

1½ cups (360 ml) coconut syrup (such as Giffard)

½ cup (120 ml) coconut milk

Demerara syrup

Combine the sugar and water in a saucepan over medium heat, stirring until the sugar has dissolved. Do not allow to boil. Remove from the heat and allow to cool. The syrup will keep, tightly sealed and refrigerated, for up to 1 month.

2 cups (440 g) demerara sugar
1 cup (240 ml) water

"Dog water" vermouth

Add all the spices to the Dolin bottle. Allow to stand overnight in the fridge.

Strain through a coffee filter and discard the solids. The mixture may be kept in the bottle, capped and refrigerated, for up to 2 weeks. (Don't forget to label the bottle!)

½ teaspoon ground nutmeg
½ teaspoon onion powder
¼ teaspoon coriander seeds
¼ teaspoon cumin seeds
750 ml bottle Dolin dry vermouth

Ginger beer

In a small saucepan, bring the water to the boil over high heat. Remove from the heat and add the grated ginger. Stir to combine, then cover and allow to stand for 1 hour.

Strain through a fine-mesh strainer, pressing the solids with the back of a spoon. Discard the solids.

Add the lime juice and sugar, stirring to dissolve the sugar. The ginger beer will keep, tightly sealed and refrigerated, for up to 1 week.

- 1 cup (240 ml) water
- 2 tablespoons finely grated fresh ginger
- ½ teaspoon lime juice, freshly squeezed
- 1 teaspoon light brown sugar

Ginger syrup

Combine the ingredients in a saucepan over low heat and stir until the sugar has dissolved. Remove from the heat and allow to cool. The syrup will keep, tightly sealed and refrigerated, for up to 1 week.

- ½ cup (120 ml) fresh ginger juice
- ½ cup (120 ml) superfine (caster) sugar

Grenadine

Combine the pomegranate juice, sugar, and pomegranate molasses in a saucepan over medium heat and stir until the sugar has dissolved. Remove from the heat and allow to cool, then stir in the orange blossom water. The grenadine will keep, tightly sealed and refrigerated, for up to 2 weeks.

- 1 cup (240 ml) pomegranate juice (such as POM Wonderful)
- 1 cup (200 g) sugar
- 1 tablespoon pomegranate molasses
- ½ teaspoon orange blossom water

Honey syrup

Combine the honey and water in a saucepan over medium heat, stirring until the honey has dissolved. Do not allow to boil. Remove from the heat and allow to cool. The syrup will keep, tightly sealed and refrigerated, for up to 1 month.

- 1 cup (340 g) honey
- 1 cup (240 ml) water

Pickled cherry tomatoes

Combine the vinegar, water, sugar, salt, pepper, and MSG in a saucepan. Bring to the boil over medium–high heat, stirring until the sugar has dissolved.

In the meantime, poke a hole in the end of each cherry tomato, using a toothpick or cocktail pick.

Place the tomatoes and garlic clove in a heatproof container, add the hot pickling mixture and allow to cool. The pickled cherry tomatoes will keep, tightly covered and refrigerated, for up to 1 month.

- 1 cup (240 ml) Champagne vinegar
- 1 cup (240 ml) water
- 1 tablespoon sugar
- 1 tablespoon kosher salt
- ½ teaspoon ground black pepper
- ¼ teaspoon MSG
- 2 cups (300 g) cherry tomatoes, washed and dried
- 1 garlic clove, peeled

Pickled onions & brine

Place the pickling spice in a tea infuser or wrap in a small square of cheesecloth (muslin). Add to a saucepan with the vinegar, water, sugar, and salt and bring to the boil. Add the onions and boil for 1 minute. Remove from the heat and allow to cool for 20–30 minutes. Discard the pickling spices.

Strain to separate the onions and the brine. Store each separately, tightly sealed and refrigerated. The onions and brine will each keep for up to 1 month.

- 1½ teaspoons pickling spice (such as McCormick)
- 2 cups (500 ml) Champagne vinegar
- 1¾ cups (420 ml) water
- 1 cup (200 g) sugar
- 1 tablespoon salt
- 8 oz (225 g) red pearl onions (about 20-25)

Raspberry syrup

1 cup (200 g) sugar

½ cup (120 ml) water

½ cup (60 g) fresh raspberries

Combine the sugar and water in a saucepan over medium heat, stirring until the sugar has dissolved. Do not allow to boil. Reduce the heat to low and add the raspberries, stirring until they begin to break down (about 5 minutes).

Remove from the heat and allow to stand for 30 minutes.

Strain the mixture through a fine-mesh strainer, discarding the solids. The syrup will keep, tightly sealed and refrigerated, for up to 2 weeks.

Rich honey syrup

1½ cups (510 g) honey

½ cup (120 ml) water

Combine the honey and water in a saucepan over medium heat, stirring until the honey has dissolved. Do not allow to boil. Remove from the heat and allow to cool. The syrup will keep, tightly sealed and refrigerated, for up to 1 month.

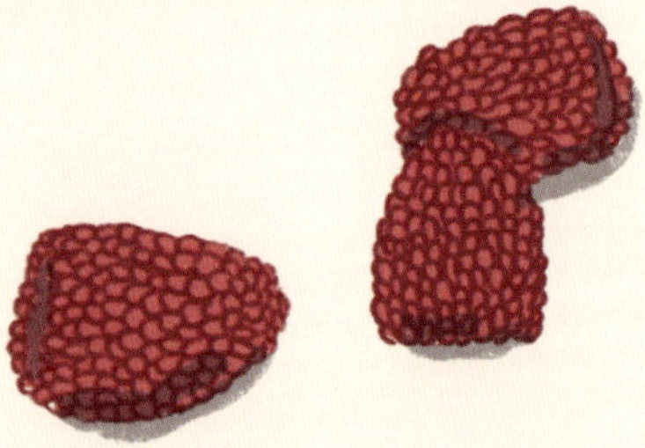

Saline solution

Heat the water, without allowing it to boil, then add the salt, stirring until the salt has dissolved. Allow to cool, then funnel into a small, clean dropper bottle.

- 2¾ oz (80 ml) water
- ¾ oz (20 g) high-quality, non-iodized salt (such as kosher or sea salt)

Simple syrup

Combine the sugar and water in a saucepan over medium heat, stirring until the sugar has dissolved. Do not allow to boil. Remove from the heat and allow to cool. The syrup will keep, tightly sealed and refrigerated, for up to 1 month.

- 1 cup (200 g) sugar
- 1 cup (240 ml) water

Index

M

N

O

P

R

S

T

V

W

Y

Smith Street Books

Published in 2026 by Smith Street Books
Naarm (Melbourne) | Australia
smithstreetbooks.com

Distributed outside of ANZ, North & Latin America by
Thames & Hudson Ltd., 6–24 Britannia Street, London, WC1X 9JD
thamesandhudson.com

EU Authorised Representative: Interart S.A.R.L.
19 rue Charles Auray, 93500 Pantin, Paris, France
productsafety@thameshudson.co.uk; www.interart.fr

ISBN: 978-1-9235-0326-7

Smith Street Books respectfully acknowledges the Wurundjeri People of the Kulin Nation, who are the Traditional Owners of the land on which we work, and we pay our respects to their Elders past and present.

Publisher: Lucy Heaver
Recipes and text: Kathryn Maier
Editor: Katri Hilden
Illustrator: Sarah Campbell
Designer: Kait Polkinghorne
Typesetter: Nikola Roberts
Proofreader: Martine Lleonart
Indexer: Helena Holmgren
Production manager: Aisling Coughlan

Printed & bound in China by C&C Offset Printing Co., Ltd.

Book 474
10 9 8 7 6 5 4 3 2 1

FSC www.fsc.org MIX Paper | Supporting responsible forestry FSC® C008047